make your
SHIFT
WORKBOOK FOR FRANCHISEES

Terrance A. Coker & Beverly D. Flaxington

ATA PRESS

DISCLAIMER

This publication is designed to provide accurate and authoritative information in regard the subject matter covered. It is sold with the understanding that the authors are not engaged in rendering legal or accounting services. If legal advice or other expert assistance is required, the services of a competent professional person should be sought.

This is not an offer to sell a franchise in any jurisdiction. This workbook is for informational purposes only. We do not give legal or accounting advice of any kind. We are not a licensed broker dealers and do not claim to be. We make no representations as to the suitability of any transaction at any time.

This overview is for informational purposes and is not an offer to sell or a solicitation of an offer to buy any franchise.

The Entrepreneur Authority LLC. is a national network of independent professional services firms, privately owned and operated by affiliates.

The Entrepreneur Authority of Michigan is an independent affiliate of The Entrepreneur Authority LLC.

Copyright © 2012, Beverly D. Flaxington & Terrance Coker. All rights reserved.

Printed in the United States of America. No part of this publication may be reproduced, stored in or introduced into a retrieval system, or transmitted, in any form, or by any means (electronic, mechanical, photocopying, recording, or otherwise) without the prior written permission of the copyright owner and the publisher of this book.

Published by ATA Press

ISBN 978-0-9837620-4-1

First printing: January 2012

All brand names and product names used in this book are trademarks, registered trademarks, or trade names of their respective holders. All statements contained herein are the opinion of the author and should not be considered professional advice.

Table of Contents

Disclaimer iii

Introduction to SHIFT Workbook 1

How to Use this Workbook 3

Introducing the S.H.I.F.T. Model™ 5

Step 1: Specify Your Desired Outcome 6

Step 2: Highlight and Categorize Obstacles 14

Step 3: Identify the Human Factor 22

Step 4: Find Alternatives 30

Step 5: Take Disciplined Action 38

Introduction to SHIFT Workbook

Are you at that transitional point in your life and asking, "Do I go into business for myself?" "What would it be like to do my own thing?" "Is owning a franchise right for me?" "What type of franchise would work best for my situation?"

Too many people make a major life decision like this one without thinking about the different aspects of their life circumstances. What do you really want to accomplish? Freedom? Control? The pride of ownership? To make a million dollars for yourself?

Before you begin the journey towards franchise ownership—or any kind of life transition—this workbook and the accompanying book, "Make Your SHIFT: The Five Most Powerful Moves You Can Make to Get Where YOU Want to Go," will provide guidance to think through some of these questions, and find the answers that are right for you. It will also lay the groundwork for working with a franchise expert.

Our goal is to help you find *your* perfect franchise.

And that's exactly what we're going to do in the next few hours… create a definition of *your* ideal type of franchise.

> per•fect adj., n. pur-fikt; v. per-fekt adjective
>
> 1. Conforming absolutely to the description or definition of an ideal type.

You are only five simple steps away from having a unique, tailored definition of an ideal type of franchise that will fit *your* lifestyle goals and financial desires. We hope you enjoy the process. If you have questions, please feel free to contact us.

Terry Coker, CEO
The Entrepreneur Authority of Michigan
Telephone: 734-459-4121 · Mobile: 734-905-1982
tcoker@eAuth.com · www.eAuth.com/Coker

Good luck as you take the first step toward a new chapter in your life.

How to Use This Workbook

This workbook has been created to work in conjunction with the bestselling book, *Make Your SHIFT: The Five Most Powerful Moves You Can Make to Get Where YOU Want to Go*, by Beverly D. Flaxington. The workbook was designed specifically for those individuals considering owning their own franchise.

It is recommended that you read one chapter of the book at a time, then complete the sections in the workbook that correspond to those chapters. We have provided you with excerpts from each chapter of the book to give an understanding and background on the S.H.I.F.T. Model™.

This workbook does not pre-suppose you will want to become a franchise owner, or what franchise you should own. In fact, the steps are designed to help you understand whether franchise ownership is right for you. If you determine that it is, it is best to work one-to-one with a seasoned eAuth.com consultant to identify the franchise that best fits your specific needs.

Try to complete the worksheets in their entirety. They are designed to ask a number of questions and help you think about issues in a strategic way. You may think you already know the answers to some questions, but may find that if you take the time to write your answers, you will uncover new information.

Introducing the S.H.I.F.T. Model™

The S.H.I.F.T. Model™ was developed based upon over two decades of experience working with individuals and businesses trying to make significant shifts. The model has five key steps:

1. **Specify the Desired Outcome:** Identify what you want and why.
2. **Highlight and Categorize Obstacles:** Find those things standing in your way and understand which ones you can control or influence.
3. **Identify the Human Factor:** Realize your own strengths and areas for improvement, and identify stakeholders in your life.
4. **Find the Alternatives:** Create a list of those options that might help you reach your Desired Outcome, overcome your obstacles, and fit your lifestyle.
5. **Take Disciplined Action:** Create your plan. Make it a step-by-step, specific process.

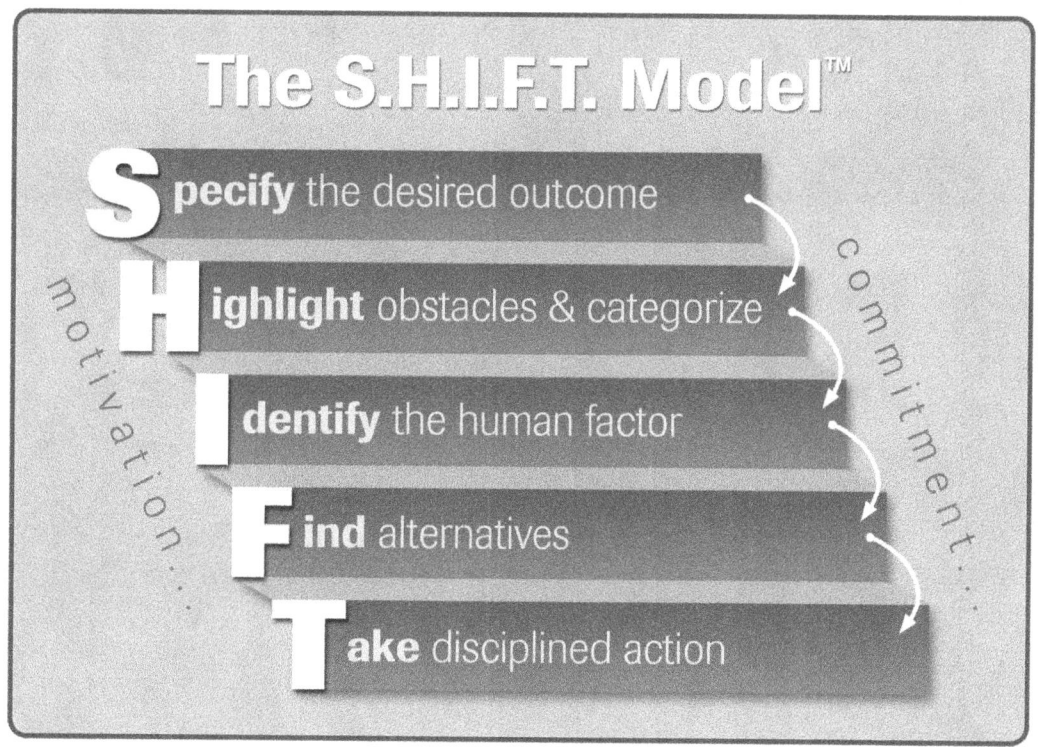

STEP 1: Specify Your Desired Outcome

ACTION STEPS

1. READ the expert notes from Chapter 1 of the book: *Make Your SHIFT: The Five Most Powerful Moves You Can Make to Get Where YOU Want to Go.*
2. COMPLETE the *State Your Desired Personal Outcomes* worksheet.
3. COMPLETE the *eAuth Worksheet: State Your Desired Business Outcomes.*

Action Step 1:
Expert Advice from Beverly Flaxington

Excerpted from *Make Your SHIFT: The Five Most Powerful Moves You Can Make to Get Where YOU Want to Go*

Specify Your Desired Outcomes

As human beings, we really are goal seeking even when the goal isn't good for us! To get truly motivated and to stay motivated, we must focus on a goal that is meaningful to us. Much of the time, though, we have an "I should" goal, a long-term goal that's hard to believe in. You know you need to define where you are going before you can make a meaningful journey. But how do we figure out what is meaningful to us? You do not have to know much about life or even individuals to reckon that most of us have very little idea about our true passions or what will make us happy. Think of all those classic romance novels in which the hero or heroine is blissfully unaware of the person in their life that is destined to make them happy. In most instances, they are unaware right up until the final scenes. And art, as they say, imitates life.

Why Does What Matters, Matter?

Why is figuring out what really matters so hard for us? It is because often we are moving away from something we do not like instead of moving toward something we do want. Couple this with the fact that we do not take into account all of the factors of who we are, and it can be a recipe for disaster when we do get what we want. Where did the adage "be careful what you wish for!" actually come from? Someone getting what they thought they wanted and finding out that "oh-oh — this isn't it!"

For example, it is not enough to hate your 9 to 5 job and decide to start a home-based business. You could set your SMART goal about this, but (among many other things) you can't actually go into business without knowing what business you want to be in. You have to know what skills you have, what impact it will have on your family, etc. Similarly, if you set a goal of "obtaining a college degree," you wouldn't want to complete a college education without knowing what degree you are going to receive and why you wanted that particular degree.

We do not do many things in life without having some sense of why we are doing them, but we rarely think deeply or even the right way about why we are doing these things.

Ask "Why?"

Depending on the "why" of your goal, how you construct your desired outcome would go deeper than merely goal setting. More than this, though, you will be able to look at your goals with a broader view, seeing the longer-term benefits and sacrifices, understanding the values that are underlying your goal and how you can incorporate them into your life most effectively.

What, then, about starting a business? Unless you have virtually unlimited resources, you can't just wake up one morning and pull a business idea out of a hat, deciding to take it upon yourself to start that type of business for yourself. You need to think carefully about the type of business that is right for you, even, perhaps especially, if you are the only person who's going to be involved in it on a daily basis. You have to ask yourself: why am I really interested in setting up my own business? After all, it is a lot of work, it takes a considerable amount of discipline, it can be very stressful. What are your desired outcomes? What do you see as possible benefits of your own business that justify the effort? Perhaps more time at home, more flexible work schedules? Maybe you are more passionate about your own business idea than you ever could be about working in a traditional 9 to 5 job, and you see your own business as a way to be happy.

Capturing desired outcomes using the S.H.I.F.T. model approach means looking at your objectives and goals in a rather holistic way. It asks you to consider the context of your life, your values and long-term preferences. When a goal is more traditionally set in a vacuum, it is likely that the goal will be met and something else may be sacrificed in the process.

Multiple Facets of Defining the Goal

Looking at your overall desired outcome allows you to take into account all of the pieces that matter to you. Don't focus too much on a single, specific goal, but you should state an outcome that is clear and measurable. That means statements like "I want to become a nicer person" or "I want to be rich" just do not cut it. You've read stories of the people who made it rich and it ruined their lives, because a singular focus on wealth can sometimes bring unintended consequences. Stories abound of the person who won the lottery, only to determine they would give it back because of all the headaches it created!

Looking at your overall desired outcome asks you to take into account all of the pieces that matter to you. You have to think about what you want your life to look like once you have made your shift and achieved the goals you are striving toward.

At this stage, identify specific goals but also write your final desired outcome as a comprehensive, clear, and understandable overall definition of what success looks like to you — and perhaps to the people who are close to you as well.

Put It In Writing!

Taking the time and being crystal clear in identifying, in writing, your desired outcomes keeps you on track once you finally create your plan (the last step in the SHIFT model).

Have you ever set out to do something and then found you were wasting time on something else? You might've been frustrated and wanting to turn your attention back to your important goal, but you were so engaged in the other thing that you couldn't do it! I found this to happen with many of the executives that I coach. We may start the week out with a clear set of desired outcomes, but then when we time track at the end of the week, the time has been spent in other areas. When that happens, I need to ask them, "Is this objective really that important to you?" Things that aren't really priorities and that won't lead to the ultimate goal will end up getting in the way, and the person I'm working with may start to feel frustrated that they have not made the progress they desire.

Having a clearly defined (and written!) set of success objectives for yourself can help you decide what you should spend time on. After all, it is easy to get distracted and spend your time and energy on things that are not really high gain activities. Think about how we can get distracted just sitting at a desk; by reading funny e-mails, or by visiting a social media site, or by chatting on the phone with someone for a long period of time. At home there is also an endless range of distractions, from household chores to the people and pets that might live with you and make demands on your time.

- Be sure to reflect back to when you stated the "why" of this goal and what matters to you about it now.
- What is the desired outcome?
- How do you define success? (Here paint the picture in as much description as possible.)
- What are the quantifiable (measurable) aspects of the goal?
- What are the qualitative aspects of the goal?
- When do you expect (or need) to meet this goal?
- What do you not want to sacrifice in meeting this goal?

Summary Section

Reflect on some of the following ideas as you complete the worksheets in this first section:

1. To get truly motivated and stay motivated, we must focus on an end goal that is meaningful to us.
2. Often we are moving away from something we do not like instead of moving toward something we do want.
3. You can't actually go into business without knowing what business you want to be in.
4. It is taking the time to create our vision of success — to be clear about the desired outcome we have for change — that we put off or never do.

Consider these questions as you complete the worksheets in this section:

1. What aspects of life are important to you?
2. If you state your overall goal only in terms of quantitative terms, you miss out on other

aspects of the kind of life you want to create.
3. Why are you really interested in setting up your own business?
4. What do you see as possible benefits of your own business that justify the effort?
5. What does success look like to you as a kind of three-dimensional entity?
6. What is the real reason for what you are trying to do?
7. First, think about what is creating your desire to make a shift in your life. What is your "why?"
8. As part of the process, think about your situation if you do not make a shift.

Action Step 2:
State Your Desired Personal Outcomes
SHIFT Model Worksheet

What is prompting me to seek this goal/desired outcome?

```
┌─────────────────────────────────────────────────┐
│                                                 │
│                                                 │
│                                                 │
│                                                 │
└─────────────────────────────────────────────────┘
```

Why do I care so much about reaching this goal?

```
┌─────────────────────────────────────────────────┐
│                                                 │
│                                                 │
│                                                 │
│                                                 │
└─────────────────────────────────────────────────┘
```

What would happen if I didn't care about this goal?

```
┌─────────────────────────────────────────────────┐
│                                                 │
│                                                 │
│                                                 │
│                                                 │
└─────────────────────────────────────────────────┘
```

Step 1: Specify Your Desired Outcome

Action Step 3:
State Your Desired Business Outcomes
eAuth tool: Your Outcomes List

Entrepreneur Authority consultants begin the search for the perfect franchise by focusing on YOU and your desired outcomes. There are no right or wrong answers. Describe the lifestyle and the financial rewards you are wanting to create through small-business ownership and, more specifically, through owning your own franchise.

E-mail your outcomes list to tcoker@eauth.com.

Write your desired outcomes for small business ownership here:

STEP 2: Highlight and Categorize Obstacles

ACTION STEPS

1. READ the expert notes from Chapter 2 of the book: *Make Your SHIFT: The Five Most Powerful Moves You Can Make to Get Where YOU Want to Go.*
2. COMPLETE the *Identify Personal Obstacles* worksheet.
3. COMPLETE the *Categorize Personal Obstacles* worksheet.
4. TAKE the *e-Quiz* (bonus tool).

Action Step 1:
Expert Advice from Beverly Flaxington

Excerpted from Make Your SHIFT: The Five Most Powerful Moves You Can Make to Get Where YOU Want to Go

Highlight and Categorize Obstacles

In the SHIFT model each step is important, but the second step often makes the difference, determining whether an individual or organization keeps doing the same thing repeatedly or has a breakthrough about what they need to do differently.

Most of us have heard the definition of "insanity"—doing the same thing over and over again but expecting a different result. But even though we intuitively understand the insanity, we stay insane too much of the time. For instance, we have the same fights with people, we engage in the same futile activities, we put the same ineffective plans into place, but somehow we think that this time we will get a different outcome from using the same approach. Then, of course, we are disappointed with ourselves and with our results because, yet again, something didn't work.

What stands in the way?

Obstacles are those things that stand in our way—the problems, the issues, the difficulties we've already had or may at some point encounter. Highlighting obstacles can be difficult, because most people do not like to be complainers and they often do not want to focus on what is, or might be, a problem somehow.

Capture, then Categorize

Never stop at simply listing your obstacles. Listing them can leave you feeling daunted by the potential trouble you will face trying to overcome them. In fact, if you just stopped at listing expected problems and left it at that, you would probably have a hard time getting up the next morning! Why bother getting out of bed when there are so many things that might stop you dead in your tracks?

The critical next step, after identifying obstacles, is to categorize them. Organize them into one of three categories:

1. Those within your control,
2. Those you cannot control but can influence, and
3. Those you cannot control.

Summary Section

Reflect on the following ideas as you complete the worksheets in this section:

1. Knowing your obstacles gives you the power to do something about them where you can, and stop wasting time over those you can't control.
2. Do not set yourself up for failure… figure out what stands in the way.
3. Without identifying the past, and without knowing what you'll encounter in the future, there is no way to put together an accurate plan.
4. Never stop at simply listing your obstacles. The critical next step, after identifying obstacles, is to categorize them.

Action Step 2:
Identify Personal Obstacles
SHIFT Model Worksheet

As I look at the desired outcome, why am I not there today? What is preventing me from reaching this goal?

List the obstacles here:

Action Step 3:
Categorize Personal Obstacles
SHIFT Model Worksheet

Obstacles within my control:

Obstacles within my sphere of influence:

Obstacles completely out of my control:

Bonus Tool:
Expert Advice from Terry Coker
The e-Quiz (e = entrepreneurial)

Many candidates express concern and confusion about where to start a franchise investigation. The Entrepreneur Authority's e-Quiz starts with you and your attitudes.

It measures independence, initiative, vision, persistence and whether or not you are a self-starter. The e-Quiz is an excellent tool to jump-start your thinking about possible outcomes and potential obstacles in determining if franchising is right for you.

The quiz is a communication tool that helps create a transparent conversation with your Entrepreneur Authority consultant, and can also be very beneficial when used to create a conversation with a spouse or business partner. We recommend you have your spouse and/or business partners take the quiz, separate from you, and then compare your score with their score to create a conversation about the similarities and the differences in your attitudes about starting a business. This is often a revealing conversation!

Your Entrepreneur Authority consultant will be interested in discussing the range of your score and the scores of those who will share profit and loss responsibilities in your business, and how that might impact whether franchising might be right for you.

The Entrepreneur Authority has assembled a set of Bonus Tools that are free for you to download and use by contacting the Entrepreneur Authority or your eAuth consultant. These electronic documents offer you and your consultant the best method to collect and communicate your confidential information in an efficient, time-sensitive manner. *Contact The Entrepreneur Authority or your eAuth consultant today.*

The Entrepreneur Authority
www.eAuth.com · 1-866-246-AUTH

Terry Coker, CEO · The Entrepreneur Authority of Michigan
Telephone: 734-459-4121 · Mobile: 734-905-1982
tcoker@eAuth.com · www.eAuth.com/Coker

STEP 3: Identify the Human Factor

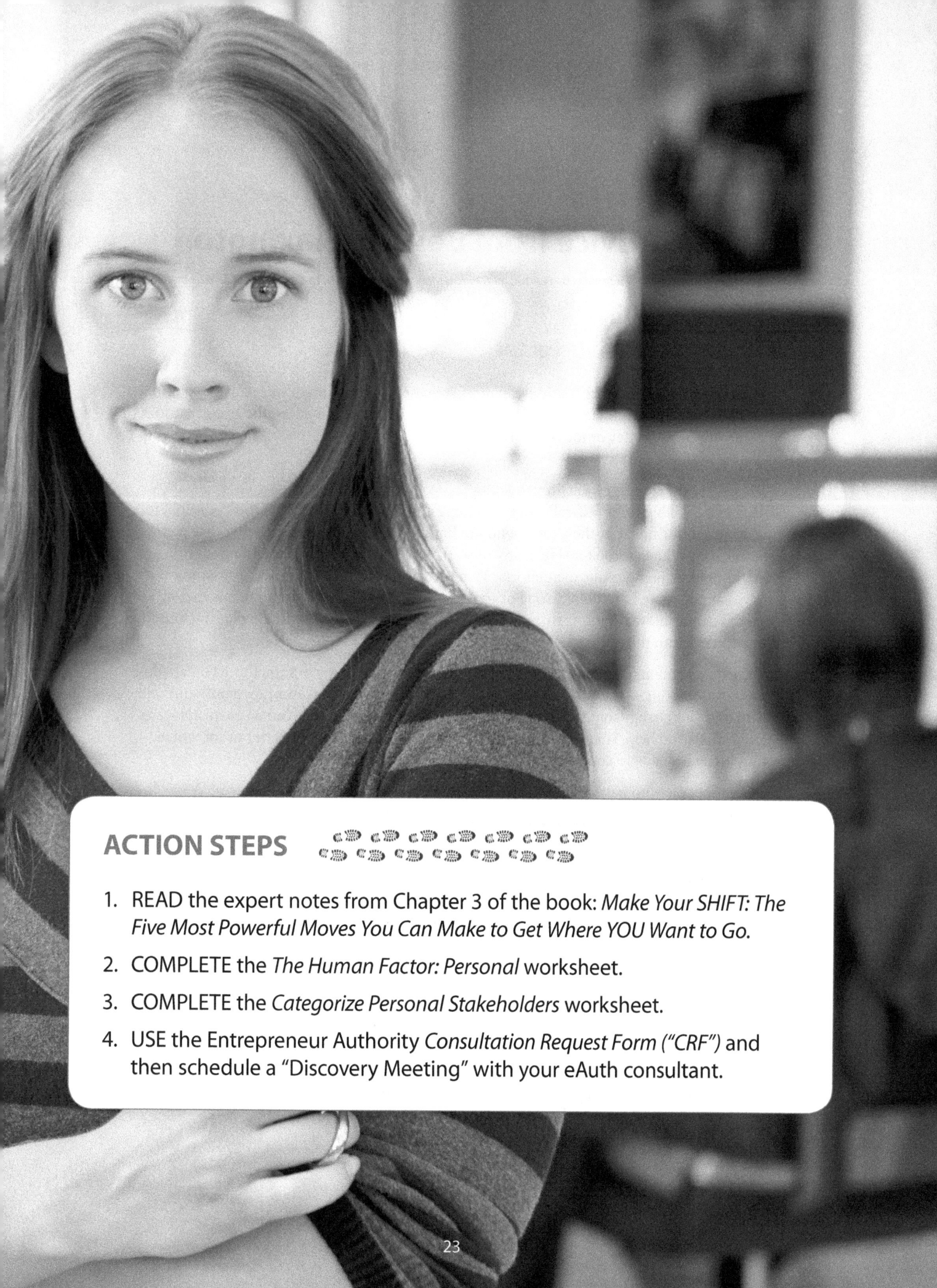

ACTION STEPS

1. READ the expert notes from Chapter 3 of the book: *Make Your SHIFT: The Five Most Powerful Moves You Can Make to Get Where YOU Want to Go.*

2. COMPLETE the *The Human Factor: Personal* worksheet.

3. COMPLETE the *Categorize Personal Stakeholders* worksheet.

4. USE the Entrepreneur Authority *Consultation Request Form ("CRF")* and then schedule a "Discovery Meeting" with your eAuth consultant.

Action Step 1:
Expert Advice from Beverly Flaxington

Excerpted from *Make Your SHIFT: The Five Most Powerful Moves You Can Make to Get Where YOU Want to Go*

Identify the Human Factor

What is the human factor? In my estimation, it is the combination of internal and external human issues. Internal factors are the ones you bring to the equation; the ones that lurk inside of you for better or for worse. External factors are the other people around you who affect you in some way.

To identify the impact of the human factor in our quest to get to our new desired state, we have to be willing to be self-reflective and honest. It is often easy, and all too common, for us to point our finger at the people who are hampering our progress or otherwise getting in our way. When we look inside, many of us have a hard time being honest about how we might help or hamper our own efforts. This isn't meant to be an exercise in bashing ourselves about all we have done wrong or to work through deeply rooted fears; it is merely an exercise in acknowledging their existence and ensuring that our ultimate plan includes a way to deal with the human impact.

The external human factors are all of those people who have a say in something you are doing or attempting — the "stakeholders" — because they have a stake in how your shift will turn out. Our change sometimes threatens others, while some people can be great advocates and give us real help. We need to know who might be involved — for better or for worse — to understand how to consider them as we create our plan for shifting.

We put people who have a stake in the change on two scales: power and interest. A low interest, low power person might be a factor but not someone who requires a lot of your time and energy. In another example, your significant other might be a high interest, high power stakeholder as you plan to quit your job and start your own business. If your significant other is actively resistant to the idea and refuses to help you in any way with the financial ramifications you can expect to encounter in your first years of trying to get the business going, they are a stakeholder with a great deal of control over your destiny and your ability to shift effectively.

A low power, high interest stakeholder — your mother, for example — may not be able to help you with the new business but might still want to hear every single thing you are doing. Although she cannot help you materially, she provides a high interest shoulder for you to lean on.

Conversely a high power, low interest person could be your landlord. He may have no interest in learning about what you are doing and why, but may exercise his or her power to keep you from running your new business out of your apartment.

Stakeholders are all around us, and if you ignore their presence at the planning stage they will somehow come into the picture as you make your shift. If they represent an obstacle, you should plan around them. If they are a positive resource, you should leverage their power and interest to help make your shift.

Summary Section

Reflect on these key ideas as you complete the worksheets:

1. Most problems in life have something to do with the human factor.
2. Having difficult people who prevent you from achieving your happiness in life is a universal experience, and the most overlooked and undervalued part of any change effort.
3. The human factor is the combination of internal issues you bring to the equation and the other people around you who affect you in some way.
4. The human factor element is often part of our obstacles process.
5. Internal factors are thoughts, feelings, education, behavioral styles, values, expertise, and emotions.
6. The external human factors are all of those people who have a say in something you are doing or attempting. Let's call them "stakeholders".
7. The most commonly used stakeholder model puts people who have a stake in the change on two scales: 1) power and 2) interest.

Action Step 2:
The Human Factor: Personal
SHIFT Model Worksheet

What internal human factors (emotions/past experiences/personal beliefs) do I identify as obstacles?

```
[                                                                    ]
```

Conversely, what internal human factors might help me make the shift?

```
[                                                                    ]
```

Action Step 3:
Categorize Personal Stakeholders
SHIFT Model Worksheet

Low Interest, High Power

High Interest, High Power

Low Interest, Low Power

High Interest, Low Power

Make Your SHIFT: Workbook For Franchisees

Bonus Tool:
Expert Advice from Terry Coker
The Consultation Request Form (CRF)

There's an old adage that says, "You never get a second chance to make a good first impression." That's the purpose of the Entrepreneur Authority's Consultation Request Form; to make a good first impression with the executives of the franchise companies you choose to conduct due diligence on. Your Entrepreneur Authority consultant will facilitate these introductions using your completed Consultation Request Form along with your current resume.

The Consultation Request Form is also a great tool to help you capture your thoughts about small business ownership. You can express your ideas regarding your ideal business model, select industry categories you have an affinity for, and deselected those categories where you don't have any interest at all. There are questions to help define your entrepreneurial fit and a spreadsheet for financial information to help everyone understand how you will fund and grow your new franchise business.

This Bonus Tool is a perfect companion to the Make Your SHIFT worksheet exercises from Chapter 3 on Identifying the Human Factor. The Consultation Request Form was designed to present you to the franchisors as a pre-qualified candidate, with realistic goals and expectations, who has given considerable thought to the idea of small business ownership. It's an excellent tool for making a good first impression!

Your Consultation Request Form is a confidential document, and its contents remain private between you and your Entrepreneur Authority consultant. The document is only sent with your permission and only to the franchise companies you choose to be introduced to, after you have given your permission.

The Entrepreneur Authority has assembled a set of Bonus Tools that are free for you to download and use by contacting the Entrepreneur Authority or your eAuth consultant. These electronic documents offer you and your consultant the best method to collect and communicate your confidential information in an efficient, time-sensitive manner. *Contact The Entrepreneur Authority or your eAuth consultant today.*

The Entrepreneur Authority
www.eAuth.com · 1-866-246-AUTH

Terry Coker, CEO · The Entrepreneur Authority of Michigan
Telephone: 734-459-4121 · Mobile: 734-905-1982
tcoker@eAuth.com · www.eAuth.com/Coker

STEP 4:
Find Alternatives

ACTION STEPS

1. READ the expert notes from Chapter 4 of the book: *Make Your SHIFT: The Five Most Powerful Moves You Can Make to Get Where YOU Want to Go.*
2. COMPLETE the *The Human Factor: Personal* worksheet.
3. COMPLETE the *Categorize Personal Stakeholders* worksheet.
4. USE the Entrepreneur Authority *Buyer's Value Matrix ("BVM")* and then read and review your customized *Recommendations Report*.

Action Step 1:
Expert Advice from Beverly Flaxington

Excerpted from *Make Your SHIFT: The Five Most Powerful Moves You Can Make to Get Where YOU Want to Go*

Find Alternatives — Your Criteria

The first important step is to establish your criteria. How will you make this very important life decision? What kinds of things will you want in place — this could include financial, family, lifestyle, location, etc.

Once you create a list of criteria, create a rating system. How do you prioritize the criteria? What is most important? Least important?

Now begin to brainstorm. Which potential options fit your important criteria? What are the pros and cons of each? How closely does each alternative match your stated Desired Outcome?

Find Alternatives — Your Solutions

Carefully review what you have done so far. Review your obstacles in their respective categories. Next, review the human factors: your internal feelings, concerns, and emotions, or the stakeholders you have identified, or both. Go through these lists and watch what your mind starts to do in terms of possible solutions. Sometimes ideas start to come together as you review your lists. If nothing comes to mind in doing this, take out a piece and write, "What can I do?" at the top of the sheet. Then list all of the things that come to your mind. Do not qualify or judge any of your ideas at first, just get everything you think of on paper.

When you later revisit your list, consider each possible solution against:

1. Your desired outcome. How do your ideas bring you closer to the outcome you desire?
2. Your obstacle list. As you look at what you can control and what you can influence, do your solutions allow you to overcome the obstacles that might be in the way?
3. Your human factor. Can you deal with this personally? Which of your stakeholders will support you in it and how?
4. Your criteria list. Which of the ideas you are considering meet your most important criteria?

Summary Section

Reflect on these key ideas as you fill out the worksheets:

1. The tendency with this step is to hear the problem or the desired outcome, and then leap directly to a solution.
2. When you start to brainstorm about your desired outcome, you need to think about your criteria.
3. Your criteria list needs to be prioritized so you are reminded of what matters to you and what factors need to be considered in your decision.
4. Criteria often include things like time, money, physical capabilities, and interest.
5. As you work on your list of criteria, think about why different criteria are important to you.
6. Before trying to determine solutions, review obstacles in each category.
7. Review the human factors before identifying personal solutions.
8. Consider each solution against the four questions.

Action Step 2:
Define Personal Criteria
SHIFT Model Worksheet

Criterion	Why is it important?	Is it a priority?

Action Step 3:
Identify Personal Solutions
SHIFT Model Worksheet

Potential Solution	Against the Desired Outcome	Control/Influence Obstacles	Human Factor	Criterion	Ranking (1-5)

Bonus Tool:
Expert Advice from Terry Coker
The Buyer's Value Matrix (BVM)

The Entrepreneur Authority's award-winning process is values driven, using *your* values.

This is what makes the process unique to each individual. Your Entrepreneur Authority consultant will start with what YOU want to achieve through small business ownership and help define the values that will create the outcomes you stated in the Make Your SHIFT exercises, and it builds on the previous eAuth Bonus Tools.

The Buyer's Values Matrix creates a single point of reference that helps to clarify both your objective needs and the emotional wants you have shared with your eAuth consultant. Your values are refined through the written exercises and the thoughtful conversation your consultant is trained to facilitate. Starting with your outcomes in writing and then filtering opportunities through your top values, this process yields a unique and tailored profile that your consultant will match to the ideal candidate profiles of franchise opportunities from our portfolio.

The single-page format of the Buyer's Values Matrix is highly effective in presenting and comparing multiple franchise opportunities against the juxtaposition of your top values. You can compare franchise companies against each other in relation to your desired outcomes in a single glance. What was confusing at the outset becomes very clear.

The exercises in Make Your SHIFT and the Entrepreneur Authority's Bonus Tools have been written to help you quantify and qualify the change management process that will help you arrive at the specific changes you are desiring to bring into your life.

The Entrepreneur Authority has assembled a set of Bonus Tools that are free for you to download and use by contacting the Entrepreneur Authority or your eAuth consultant. These electronic documents offer you and your consultant the best method to collect and communicate your confidential information in an efficient, time-sensitive manner. *Contact The Entrepreneur Authority or your eAuth consultant today.*

The Entrepreneur Authority
www.eAuth.com · 1-866-246-AUTH

Terry Coker, CEO · The Entrepreneur Authority of Michigan
Telephone: 734-459-4121 · Mobile: 734-905-1982
tcoker@eAuth.com · www.eAuth.com/Coker

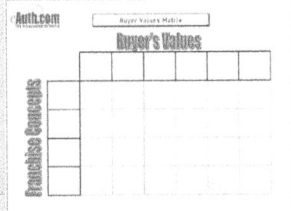

STEP 5: Take Disciplined Action

ACTION STEPS

1. READ the expert notes from Chapter 5 of the book: *Make Your SHIFT: The Five Most Powerful Moves You Can Make to Get Where YOU Want to Go.*

2. USE the Entrepreneur Authority tool *The Action Register* and schedule Introductions to Franchise Companies with your eAuth consultant.

3. COMPLETE the *Breaking Down the Details* worksheet.

Action Step 1:
Expert Advice from Beverly Flaxington

Excerpted from *Make Your SHIFT: The Five Most Powerful Moves You Can Make to Get Where YOU Want to Go*

Take Disciplined Action

This is the step where action is required. In order to get where YOU want to go, you must develop the plan. The plan should have clear steps, with timeframes associated with each one. It's also the time to look around and see who else needs to be involved, or could offer help at any step.

Don't move on until you have broken down your plan into manageable steps and listed each of the steps clearly and in order.

Summary Section

Reflect on these key ideas before you complete the worksheets:

- Now it is time to create your plan. This is the most difficult part of the process, because in most situations, the devil is in the details.
- Ask yourself how, exactly, do you plan to implement your solution?
- The disciplined part comes down to actually taking responsibility and staying focused on your desired outcomes.
- The only people who actually make change happen are those who can clearly identify what steps they will take in order to get them to their desired outcomes.
- Each step in the process should be broken down into its finest level of detail so that nothing is left to assumption.
- The process of breaking down the plan into specific, discrete steps is where you finally take your disciplined action.
- So, make your commitment. Create your plan. Find a way to keep yourself on track and make your shift happen!

Step 5: Take Disciplined Action

Action Step 3:
Breaking Down the Details
SHIFT Model Worksheet

Discrete step in the process	Who will do this?	By when?	Is there a cost? If so, how much?	What else needs to be considered at this step?

Bonus Tool:
Expert Advice from Terry Coker
The Action Register

The final chapter of *Make Your SHIFT* is titled "Take Disciplined Action" and that's the exact purpose of the Entrepreneur Authority's Action Register: to give you a step-by-step action guide to finding a franchise that matches your unique and specific values.

When you have put your outcomes on paper, considered any obstacles that may arise, defined the values that drive your search, and considered the human factors involved, you can begin with confidence to take action because you now know exactly what you are searching for and what it will look like when you find it. "Guesswork" has been eliminated.

You can rapidly move through multiple opportunities, both inside the franchise world and outside of small business ownership, as you compare what a business model might be capable of delivering against what you desire to create for you and your family.

The work with your Entrepreneur Authority consultant is far from over; in fact it's just beginning. Your eAuth consultant will facilitate the introductions to the franchise companies you have selected and stay with you through the entire due diligence process until you have made your decisions about each franchise company you choose to investigate. Your eAuth consultant can provide additional legal, financial, and small business resources in addition to guiding you through the steps in the Action Register.

The Entrepreneur Authority has assembled a set of Bonus Tools that are free for you to download and use by contacting the Entrepreneur Authority or your eAuth consultant. These electronic documents offer you and your consultant the best method to collect and communicate your confidential information in an efficient, time-sensitive manner. *Contact The Entrepreneur Authority or your eAuth consultant today.*

The Entrepreneur Authority
www.eAuth.com · 1-866-246-AUTH

Terry Coker, CEO · The Entrepreneur Authority of Michigan
Telephone: 734-459-4121 · Mobile: 734-905-1982
tcoker@eAuth.com · www.eAuth.com/Coker

Congratulations! You have completed all of the workbook exercises. Contact your local eAuth expert to talk in more detail about whether franchising, and what franchise, is right for you.

The Entrepreneur Authority
www.eAuth.com · 1-866-246-AUTH (2884)

Terry Coker, CEO
The Entrepreneur Authority of Michigan
O: 734-459-4121 · M: 734-905-1982
tcoker@eAuth.com · www.eAuth.com/Coker

www.ingramcontent.com/pod-product-compliance
Lightning Source LLC
Chambersburg PA
CBHW081023040426
42444CB00014B/3326